AFRICAN-AMERICAN HOLIDAYS

by Faith Winchester

Reading Consultant:
Harvey H. Alston

Bridgestone Books
an Imprint of Capstone Press

Fast Facts

• All blacks have ancestors from the continent of Africa.
• More than 30 million African Americans live in the United States.
• African Americans are a minority group in the United States, but they are a majority group in some cities.
• African-American culture has contributed much to art, music, literature, and religion in North America.

Bridgestone Books are published by Capstone Press • 818 North Willow Street, Mankato, Minnesota 56001
Copyright © 1996 by Capstone Press • All rights reserved • Printed in the United States of America

Library of Congress Cataloging-in-Publication Data
Winchester, Faith.
    African-American holidays/by Faith Winchester.
    p. cm.--(Read-and-discover ethnic holidays)
    Includes bibliographical references and index.
    Summary: Discusses special times of the year when African Americans celebrate, including Black History Month, Juneteenth, Harambee, Junkanoo, and Kwanzaa.
    ISBN 1-56065-456-2
    1. Holidays--United States--Juvenile literature. 2. Afro-Americans--Social life and customs--Juvenile literature. [1. Holidays. 2. Afro-Americans--Social life and customs..] I. Title. II. Series
GT4803.A2W55 1996
394.2'6'08996073--dc20
                                     96-25910
                                       CIP
                                       AC

Photo credits
Unicorn/Aneal Vohra, cover.; 4; Jean Higgins, 8; Jeff Greenberg, 18.
FPG, 6, 20, Archive Photos, 10. Bob Daemmrich, 12.
Peter Ford, 14. Beryl Goldberg, 16.

Table of Contents

Words in **boldface** type in the text are defined in the Words to Know section in the back of this book.

African Americans

African Americans have a rich history. They are proud of their culture. African Americans were once slaves. They were not allowed to celebrate their holidays the way they wanted. But they kept remembering their culture. They kept it alive by telling their children stories. Today, they celebrate any way they want.

Many African-American holidays are fairly new. They remember parts of their history. Some holidays honor famous people. Others celebrate events or ideas. African Americans use holidays to celebrate their many **triumphs**.

African Americans have their roots in Africa. It is a continent made up of 54 countries. African cloth called kente (ken-tay) is an expression of their culture. It is bright and colorful. Many African Americans wear kente cloth to show life and action.

African-American holidays celebrate many black triumphs.

Martin Luther King Jr.'s Birthday

Martin Luther King Jr. was an African-American leader and minister. He worked to make people see that African Americans were their equals. King was born on January 15, 1929.

King wanted equal treatment for blacks. He led marches and made speeches. King believed in keeping peace. He did not want to fight. He believed voting was the way to bring change. He gave a famous speech in Washington, D.C. It is called "I have a dream." King had a dream that blacks and whites would come to respect each other.

King was killed on April 4, 1968. People remember King on the third Monday of January. This was made an official holiday in 1983 by President Ronald Reagan. African Americans think about King's work for peace and equality. They read his famous dream speech and have parades. They remember this great man with respect.

Martin Luther King Jr. Day was made an official holiday in 1983.

Black History Month

February is Black History Month. African Americans remember how they have survived hard times. All Americans recognize Black History Month, not just blacks.

During Black History Month, children learn about famous African Americans. Many libraries and museums have special displays and activities. It is a month to learn about and remember what African Americans have added to American culture.

African Americans have shaped much of America's musical history. They created jazz, the blues, and rap music. Gospel music and spirituals got their start in African-American churches.

For African Americans, culture is more than music, art, and food. It is everything they do and believe. African-American culture is a way of thinking. They think about cooperation and family. Black History Month is a time to learn and think.

Some African Americans dress in native clothes for art festivals.

Malcolm X's Birthday

Malcolm X was an African-American religious and political leader. He wanted blacks to be equal to whites. He was not always as peaceful as Martin Luther King Jr. He wanted to be equal even if it meant having to fight.

Malcolm X was born on May 19, 1925, in Omaha, Nebraska. He was named Malcolm Little. Malcolm changed his name to X when he was older. He said Little was a slave name. Malcolm was a **Muslim**. His strong ideas got him into trouble. Muslim leaders wanted nothing to do with him. They told him to stop spreading his ideas.

On February 21, 1965, Malcolm X was killed. His ideas live on in a book. It is called *The Autobiography of Malcolm X*.

African Americans celebrate Malcolm X's birthday on May 19. Many communities have parades. They remember his fights for freedom.

African Americans remember Malcolm X and his fights for freedom.

Juneteenth

Juneteenth is a holiday to remember when African Americans were freed from slavery. Juneteenth celebrates the day in June when the slaves in Texas were freed. It is celebrated on the Saturday closest to June 19.

Other freedom celebrations are held at different times in different places. The day they are celebrated depends on when the slaves were freed in a certain place. January 1 is celebrated often, too. It is called Emancipation Day. This was the day the southern slaves were freed by President Abraham Lincoln in 1863.

African Americans celebrate their freedom with parades and speeches. They give sermons and sing. They have picnics and games. At the beginning of the day, they read the law Lincoln signed. It is called the Emancipation Proclamation. The holiday lasts all day and into the night.

This Juneteenth parade in Austin, Texas, celebrates the freeing of the slaves.

Marcus Garvey's Birthday

Marcus Garvey was born on August 17, 1887, in Jamaica. He moved to the United States to start an organization called the Universal Negro Improvement Association (UNIA). Garvey devoted his life to UNIA. He wanted all African Americans to return to Africa. He thought they would have better lives in the country of their **ancestors**.

Garvey created the saying, "Black is beautiful." He created the Liberation Flag. It is also called the bendera. This flag has three stripes. They are red, black, and green. Black stands for the color of the people. Red stands for their struggle. Green means the future or a reward.

The bendera is a great symbol for African Americans. It is their special flag. Many hang it outside their homes on Garvey's birthday.

Garvey was sent away from the United States by the government in 1927. He died in 1940 in England.

The bendera, created by Marcus Garvey, is an important part of all African-American celebrations.

Harambee

Harambee is the African-American **alternative** to Halloween. Harambee means "unity" in Swahili, the main language in Africa.

Harambee was started by African Americans in Dallas, Texas. They wanted to have one big party. So they started a new holiday. It takes place on October 31, the same day as Halloween.

No one goes door-to-door for treats during Harambee. They all bring treats to one place. That way everyone can be together.

Art is very important at the Harambee party. There are sculptures, paintings, and more. The art is always done by black artists. Everyone tries to learn what the artist is saying with the art.

The party includes plays, films, music and dance. Harambee is time to learn about African-American art and culture. Some African Americans choose to celebrate Harambee instead of Halloween.

Harambee is like Halloween, but the treats are all in one place.

Junkanoo

Junkanoo is an old holiday. It was started by the slaves. They were not allowed to celebrate Christmas on December 25. They were too busy working. They could not celebrate Christmas until December 26.

Junkanoo is the black Christmas. It lasts from December 26 to January 1. The main event of this holiday is a band competition. Bands practice in secret. They make special costumes.

During Junkanoo, the bands show off their costumes and play their special music. They march in a long parade. There are prizes for the band with the best music and the most colorful and detailed costumes. It takes months for the bands to practice and get their costumes just right.

Junkanoo is celebrated in North America, the Bahamas, Trinidad, and Jamaica. In some places, it has been replaced by Kwanzaa.

Junkanoo is full of colorful costumes and fun music.

Kwanzaa

Kwanzaa celebrates all black people in the world. It is a celebration of ideas. Kwanzaa lasts from December 26 to January 1. Each day honors an idea for African Americans to live by.

Kwanzaa was started by an African American named Maulana Karenga. He wanted African Americans to be proud. He created a holiday just for blacks.

Seven is an important number for Kwanzaa. There are seven principles to follow. There are seven symbols on a Kwanzaa **altar**. The holiday is seven days long. Even the word has seven letters.

Kwanzaa is a time for families to be together. They read one principle each day. The principles are about unity, work, and creativity. They are meant to help African Americans be better people. On the last night of Kwanzaa, there is a feast called karamu. Everyone brings food to share. It is a special time.

African families get together around the Kwanzaa altar.

Hands On: Make a Sculpture

During Harambee, African Americans focus on art. One form of African-American art is sculpture. You can make a sculpture out of a special dough. Your sculpture can look like whatever you want. Be creative.

You will need
- 1/2 cup (.12 liters) salt
- 3/4 cup (.18 liters) boiling water
- 2 cups (.48 liters) nonrising flour
- 1 tablespoon (15 milliliters) vegetable oil
- cookie sheet covered with aluminum foil

1. Put the salt in a large bowl. Add the boiling water. Stir until the salt disolves. Let the mixture cool for a few minutes.
2. Add the flour and oil to the bowl. Mix all the ingredients together.
3. Put a small amount of oil on your hands. This will keep the dough from sticking to them while you sculpt.
4. Take the dough out of the bowl and kneed it with your hands. This will take out any air bubbles and make it easier to work with.
5. Mold the dough into whatever form you want. Your sculpture can be as simple or as complicated as you like.
6. Put your finished sculpture on the cookie sheet. Bake it in an oven preheated to 300 degrees Fahrenheit (149 degrees Celsius). Bake your sculpture until it looks dry. Large sculptures may take two hours or more. Smaller sculptures will take less time.
7. When your sculpture is out of the oven and cool, you may want to paint it with paints. Or you can add food coloring to the dough when you mix it. Remember, the color will fade when you bake it.

Pronunciation Guide

bendera	ben-dare-rah
Emancipation	ee-man-suh-pay-shun
Harambee	hair-um-bee
Junkanoo	junk-uh-new
karamu	kah-rah-moo
Kwanzaa	kwan-zah
Swahili	swah-he-lee

Words to Know

altar—table that holds holy things
ancestor—relative who came before
alternative—something that can be chosen instead
Muslim—one who follows the religion of Islam
triumph—have victory over

Read More

Cohen, Hennig and Tistram Potter Coffin. *America Celebrates!* Chicago: Visible Ink Press, 1991.

Hintz, Martin and Kate Hintz. *Kwanzaa: Why We Celebrate It the Way We Do*. Mankato, Minn.: Capstone Press, 1996.

Steele, Philip. *Festivals Around the World*. Minneapolis: Dillon Press, 1986.

Westridge Young Writer's Workshop. *Kids Explore America's African-American Heritage*. Sante Fe, N.M.: John Muir Publications, 1992.

Useful Addresses and Internet Sites

America's Black Holocaust Museum
2233 North Fourth Street
Milwaukee, WI 53212

Afro-American Cultural Foundation
10 Fiske Place, Suite 204-206
Mount Vernon, NY 10550

Kwanzaa Information Center
http://www.melanet.com/melanet/kwanzaa/
Happy Birthday, Dr King
http://buckman.pps.k12.or.us/King/King.html

Index